JIM BURNS

POEMS FOR TRIBUNE

For Norman Schwenk.
Keep the faith
for these times will surely pass
Jim Burns

WIDE SKIRT PRESS, 1988

WAITING FOR XMAS

Xmas soon, and the glossy war books
are piled high in the shops,
waiting to be wrapped as presents.

Xmas soon, and toy tanks and soldiers
are lined up on the counters,
waiting to delight the children.

Xmas soon, and all the best war films
are scheduled into key spots,
waiting to entertain the families.

Xmas soon, and the message is peace,
and good will to all men, and I am
waiting for it to get through.

December 26, 1975

SONG FOR SECTARIANS

We entered the year of '76
with capitalism in decline.
I decided to help it on its way
and sign on that dotted line.

I joined up with the IMG
and got into the fray,
but there was a disagreement
and I moved along the way.

I gave my all to the WRP,
and held the banner high
until we fell on policy,
and they purged me as a spy.

The SWP were next on my list,
I sailed into their fight,
then we hit a point of principle
and I suddenly saw the light.

I moved over to the RSL,
and then to the RCP.
I even tried the YMCA,
but it wasn't right for me.

So I opened a small office,
and the plaque upon the wall
had the letters IWRSL,
and "Soon may Capitalism fall."

I issued an eight-page paper
which attacked the other groups,
then put out a call for members
and waited for my troops.

A year later there were ten of us,
and there would have been more,
but we had a factional struggle
and expelled the other four.

But we carried on our striving
towards the great change
by fighting the left-wing parties
that came within our range.

And now the group I founded
has purged me from its ranks,
and for my early efforts
never a word of thanks.

But I'll show them I'm strong,
I'll bring about their fall.
I'll sign with the Special Branch,
and inform on them all.

January 9, 1976

WITH THE LIBERALS

"Yes," she said, "There's this new museum,
and they have relics of the labour struggles,
with strike leaflets, and badges, and
union banners, and Keir Hardie's mining lamp."
Ah, I thought, Keir Hardie's lamp, and I
caught a glimpse of hungry women and children,
and an echo of impassioned speeches, and the
unfinished fight for freedom from wage slavery.

"It's so wonderful to look back on the past,"
she continued, "And of course, we always voted
Labour until recently, but when they brought in
those last measures, and we couldn't afford
the new car, it really was too much.
You do understand, don't you? One's heart is
still in the right place, but one has to live."
The lamp flickered fitfully in the dark.

April 30, 1976

SNAPSHOTS FROM MAY, 1926

(The General Strike took place
in Britain in May, 1926)

Three pretty girls in gay hats
sit around a garden table,
feeding cream cakes to a pekinese.

Several women in shabby shawls
cluster at a street corner,
children clinging to their skirts.

Two fresh-faced youths in sweaters
smile bravely from a bus,
a policeman perched behind them.

A dozen sullen men in worn suits
stand, hands in pockets,
staring at an armoured car.

Snapshots from fifty years ago,
the smooth surfaces cracking,
and the bitterness seeping through.

May 7, 1976

HISTORY LESSON

The First World War was staged
so that the Hovis advertisements
can now show a soldier coming home
to cobbled streets and brown bread.

The Second World War took place
so that television companies
can easily fill endless hours
with re-runs of the better bits.

The Third World War will happen
so that a sandwich-munching public
can be fried to a crispy finish
in front of the flickering screens.

June 4, 1976

UNEMPLOYED

The politicians made speeches to the
businessmen, and they listened
with interest, but the dole queues
grew a little longer each week.
Not that anyone cared. They were invisible,
those people signing to say they hadn't
worked, or otherwise earned anything.
They drew enough to dress tidily,
meet some of the bills, pay the rent,
and feed their children. No-one thought
of them as unusual. Perhaps they
couldn't afford to have a holiday,
possibly they were sometimes more morose
than others, and kept their hands
in their pockets and stopped smoking.
But their bitterness never massed itself
in ranks, so no-one worried. They were
always around, but no-one saw them.
They could just as well have been dead.

June 17, 1977

SCHOOL DAYS

I remember we sat in a cold room,
and she read a story about a missionary
who, when he saw his first savage,
said, "Mass, I saw it," and the native
proudly adopted the name, "Massasoit,"
and followed the missionary around,
helping him in his efforts to convert
the other savages, and bring them
the benefits of the white man's ways.
That was towards the end of 1943,
and the civilised nations of the world
were busily killing millions of people
with skill and efficiency and flair.

August 10, 1977

RAMON MERCADER'S EPITAPH

(Mercader, Trotsky's assassin,
was reported to have died in
Havana, October 18th, 1978.)

It was a job well done,
even if I did get caught
and sentenced to twenty years
in a Mexican prison.
What are twenty years?
Trotsky's achievements
in the Revolution, his books,
his ideas, will be remembered,
but then, so will I.
His life may have been
a brilliant, dynamic chapter,
but I had the last word.
My mediocrity triumphed
in the long run. History
will never be able to deny it.

December 15, 1978

TRAVELLING THROUGH TIME

I read about the Thirties on the train,
strikes, unemployment, fascism, Spain.
Outside the window the grey sky drips,
the melting snow flecks the dirty tips.
The shuttered factories and empty shops
scar the streets at every stop,
there are violent slogans, a foot tall,
and "Vote NF" on a warehouse wall.
Some affluence, too, with streams of cars,
and flashing lights on endless bars,
but the bookstall placards catch my eye,
in Spain, they tell us, people die.
And here's a picket, another row,
but no need to worry about that just now.
I turn my attention back to the book,
the mirror of history is where I look.
Strikes, unemployment, fascism, Spain.
I read about the Thirties on the train.

February 23, 1979

THE DISTANT LOOK

I once saw a photograph of Eugene Victor Debs,
old American socialist, taken towards the end of his life
when he was, they said, drunk and disillusioned.
Lined face, bald head, and a distant look in his eyes
that spoke a thousand words about lost hopes,
betrayals, and the deaths of his greatest dreams.
He was sitting on the steps of a courthouse,
uselessly protesting against one more injustice.

And somehow, on that photograph, he was like my father,
another tired old man, sitting in a small backyard,
gazing for hours at the sky. Which of his dreams had we
shattered? What hopes had we destroyed with sneers?
How many times had we betrayed him, and justified it
for our causes? Old men, whatever the reasons
you sat there, staring into space, don't forever haunt me
with your distant looks. I'm too afraid of my own.

March 30, 1979

TRUE CONFESSION

"The book was freely available, but why, he asked would anyone want it other than for an unlawful purpose? - newspaper report of the words of prosecuting counsel in the Old Bailey trial of alleged anarchists."

I bought it in a bookshop,
it's the truth, I swear on my soul.
I didn't know that it was evil,
or I wouldn't have bought it at all.

I know there are things about books
that are dark and dangerous and grim,
and I accept that just to buy them
is evidence of a great crime.

I'm sorry I made such a blunder,
and I'll never do it again.
I promise to mend my wicked ways,
and, in future, watch television.

I'll now make my final confession
about that unlawful purpose. You see,
I bought the book just to read it.
I beg that the Court will forgive me.

November 16, 1979

THE GRAVE FACE

You should start to feel worried
when the human race puts on its grave face.
Flags fly, anthems strike up,
and, given the right circumstances,
people will quickly begin to die.
They may already have died, of course,
when the grave face is on display,
though the music will be slightly different,
and the flags a little lower.
So, always beware of the grave face.
When it's around
you're either in your grave, or soon will be.

November 30, 1979

SEVEN MINUTES TO GO

"An accelerating drift towards nuclear holocaust has led the international body of nuclear scientists to move the hands of their symbolic doomsday clock to seven minutes to midnight."

There really isn't much
you can do in seven minutes.
You can curse a few people,
kiss a few others, wonder
where the kids are, and worry
about whether or not your wife
will manage to catch a bus home.
You can also do a simple thing,
such as make a cup of tea,
or you can switch on the radio
to see if they cover the event.
It is probably best that you
do something or other, so that
your mind will be occupied,
and you won't get too depressed.
To repeat, there isn't much
that you can do in seven minutes,
but anything is better
than merely watching the clock.

March 28, 1980

THINGS TO COME

"Television at breakfast in new contract proposals"

You may wake up and wonder
just what to do each day
without a job or money,
but think of the pleasure
you'll derive from television.
Advertisements for holidays
in exotic places, programmes
about beautiful homes,
assurances that better times
are just around the corner,
and advice on how to invest.
You can take it all in
as you make a cup of coffee,
and reflect on the fact
that you're not going far,
but that tomorrow you'll get
King Kong with your cornflakes.

May 2, 1980

FOR AN OLD COMRADE

I thought that you
would always be there,
and that when I went back,
and walked through the streets,
I'd hear your voice
call my name.

And I imagined
that I would never forget
which pub to find you in,
so that we could drink,
and talk about jazz
and books and socialism.

I hoped that somehow
we'd share a store of memories,
and that we would laugh
about the times we'd known,
and wonder together
about friends who were gone.

And then the letter arrived
to say that you had died.
These are the days
when such news comes too often,
and all that is solid
melts into air.

May 25, 1984

REPORT FROM EAST BERLIN

When the People's Police
in the People's State
ordered the people to disperse,
they refused
and stood their ground.
The People's Police then charged
and drove them along
the Unter den Linden,
with the people all the time
singing The Internationale.
The report does not say
which song, if any,
the People's Police sang.

June 26, 1987

HAVE A NICE DAY

My companion, a social worker,
informs me that her clients
seem to beat their children less
when the weather is warm.
Some men, on the other hand,
assault their wives more,
a practice she attributes
to the effects of drinking beer
in the heat of the sun.

She says it lightly,
as if to construct a defence
against the endless distress
she has to deal with.
I look out of the window,
and watch the clouds clearing
to let the blue shine through.
I do not have the heart
to tell her to have a nice day.

July 17, 1987

IF YOU WANT TO KNOW THE TIME

I remember the days
when the seaside stalls
sold a comic policeman's hat
that perched on top
of a child's head
as an object of good humour.

Now they stock
a shiny black riot helmet
that fits snugly and looks real.
And a seven year old
scowling from behind a visor
has me worried.

September 25, 1987

AMUSING OURSELVES TO DEATH

Let's not be serious
when we meet,
we don't want to seem so dull.

Who knows a good story,
who'll buy more wine?
While all around, all the time,

the streets are dirtier,
there's rising crime,
the poorest beg and the rich consume.

But let's have a good laugh,
and plenty of fun,
go on holiday, get some sun.

But, please, don't be serious,
don't take things to heart.
It may just stop before it breaks.

August 12, 1988

POEMS FOR TRIBUNE

ISBN 1 870505 13 1

Published by Wide Skirt Press
93 Blackhouse Road
Fartown
Huddersfield
West Yorkshire
HD2 1AP

Layout and design by Geoff Hattersley
Printed at Monteney, Sheffield

The dates beneath the poems in this collection indicate their original publication in Tribune.